A Beginning-to-Read Book

Saving Money

by Mary Lindeen

NORWOOD HOUSE PRESS

DEAR CAREGIVER,

The *Beginning to Read—Read and Discover* books provide emergent readers the opportunity to explore the world through nonfiction while building early reading skills. The text integrates both common sight words and content vocabulary. These key words are featured on lists provided at the back of the book to help your child expand his or her sight word recognition, which helps build reading fluency. The content words expand vocabulary and support comprehension.

Nonfiction text is any text that is factual. The Common Core State Standards call for an increase in the amount of informational text reading among students. The Standards aim to promote college and career readiness among students. Preparation for college and career endeavors requires proficiency in reading complex informational texts in a variety of content areas. You can help your child build a foundation by introducing nonfiction early. To further support the CCSS, you will find Reading Reinforcement activities at the back of the book that are aligned to these Standards.

Above all, the most important part of the reading experience is to have fun and enjoy it!

Sincerely,

Shannon Cannon

Shannon Cannon, Ph.D.
Literacy Consultant

Norwood House Press • P.O. Box 316598 • Chicago, Illinois 60631
For more information about Norwood House Press please visit our website at
www.norwoodhousepress.com or call 866-565-2900.
© 2016 Norwood House Press. Beginning-to-Read™ is a trademark of Norwood House Press.
All rights reserved. No part of this book may be reproduced or utilized in any form or by any
means without written permission from the publisher.

Editor: Judy Kentor Schmauss

Designer: Lindaanne Donohoe

Photo Credits:

Shutterstock, cover, 1, 3, 6-7, 8-9, 10-11, 12, 13, 14-15, 22-23, 26-27, 28-29;
Dreamstime, 4-5 (©JonothanRoss), 18-19 (©Edbockstock), 20-21 (©Johnkwan);
iStock, 16-17, 24, 25

Library of Congress Cataloging-in-Publication Data
    Lindeen, Mary.
     Saving money / by Mary Lindeen.
        pages cm. – (A beginning to read book)
     Audience: K to Grade 3.
     Summary: "You can save money at home or you can take it to a bank. Find out how the
    bank keeps your money safe. Learn about coins and bills and howto save, spend, and
    share them. This title includes reading activities and a word list"– Provided by publisher.
     ISBN 978-1-59953-699-6 (library edition : alk. paper)
     ISBN 978-1-60357-784-7 (ebook)
     1. Finance, Personal–Juvenile literature. 2. Saving and investment–Juvenile literature. I. Title.
    HG179.L5116 2015
    332.024–dc23
                     2015001008

Manufactured in the United States of America in Stevens Point, Wisconsin. 275N-062015

Do you have any money?

You can save it.

You can put it in a bank.

People put their money in a bank to keep it safe.

This bank is small.

You can keep it in your house.

See the hole at
the top?

Put your money
in here.

See the hole at the bottom?

Get your money out here.

This bank is big.

Many people work here.

They can help you save your money.

They can keep your money safe.

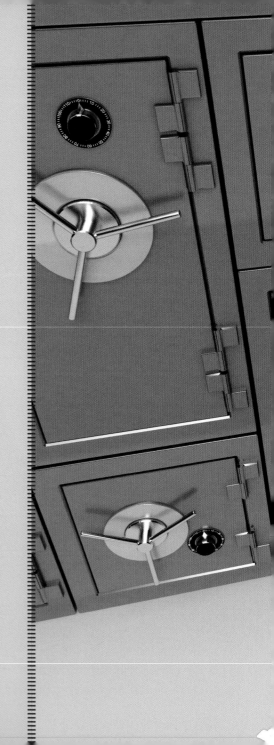

You can give
them coins.

You can give
them bills.

They will put it in the vault.

Your money will be safe here.

aily Balance Su

Balance($)

$53.99

Market S

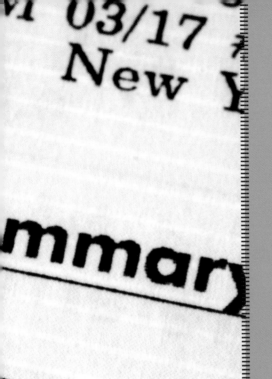

The bank helps you keep track of your money.

They send you a report like this every month.

It shows how much money you have in the bank.

Do you want to buy something?

You will need money.

Go to the bank.

Ask the teller for your money.

Here is your money.

You saved it.

Now you can spend it or share it.

Look at all of this money!

What will you do with it?

...READING REINFORCEMENT...

CRAFT AND STRUCTURE

To check your child's understanding of this book, recreate the following diagram on a sheet of paper. Read the book with your child, and then help him or her fill in the diagram using what they learned. Work together to identify what your child now knows about saving money and what else he or she still wants to know about it.

What I Know About Saving Money	
What I Still Want to Know About Saving Money	

VOCABULARY: Learning Content Words

Content words are words that are specific to a particular topic. All of the content words for this book can be found on page 32. Use some or all of these content words to complete one or more of the following activities:

- Help your child find pairs of content words that have something in common, either in meaning, structure, or both.

- Create a word web for one or more of the content words. Write the word itself in the center of the web, and synonyms (words with similar meanings), antonyms (words with opposite meanings), or other related words in the outer spokes.

- Have your child identify a content word by using three clues you provide; for example, *person, bank, help→teller*.

- Help your child make word cards: On each card, have him or her write a content word, draw a picture to illustrate the word, and write a sentence using the word.

- Help your child find content words from this book in other written materials in your home.

FOUNDATIONAL SKILLS: Pronouns

Pronouns are words used in place of nouns (people, places, things, or ideas). Have your child identify which words are pronouns in the list below. Then help your child find pronouns in this book.

you	save	bank	they
money	it	she	need

CLOSE READING OF NONFICTION TEXT

Close reading helps children comprehend text. It includes reading a text, discussing it with others, and answering questions about it. Use these questions to discuss this book with your child:

- What is a bank?
- How would you explain what a bank report is?
- What questions would you ask a bank teller?
- What are the good and bad things about saving money?
- How is saving money at home the same as saving money at a bank?
- Are you a money saving, sharing, or spending person?

FLUENCY

Fluency is the ability to read accurately with speed and expression. Help your child practice fluency by using one or more of the following activities:

- Reread this book to your child at least two times while he or she uses a finger to track each word as you read it.
- Read the first sentence aloud. Then have your child reread the sentence with you. Continue until you have finished this book.
- Ask your child to read aloud the words they know on each page of this book. (Your child will learn additional words with subsequent readings.)
- Have your child practice reading this book several times to improve accuracy, rate, and expression.

··· Word List ···

Saving Money uses the 68 words listed below. *High-frequency* words are those words that are used most often in the English language. They are sometimes referred to as sight words because children need to learn to recognize them automatically when they read. *Content words* are any words specific to a particular topic. Regular practice reading these words will enhance your child's ability to read with greater fluency and comprehension.

High-Frequency Words

a	get	it	put	to
all	give	like	see	want
ask	go	look	show(s)	what
at	have	many	small	will
be	help(s)	much	something	with
big	here	now	the	work
can	house	of	their	you
do	how	or	them	your
every	in	out	they	
for	is	people	this	

Content Words

bank	coins	month	save(d)	teller
bills	hole	need	send	top
bottom	keep	report	share	track
buy	money	safe	spend	vault

··· About the Author

Mary Lindeen is a writer, editor, parent, and former elementary school teacher. She has written more than 100 books for children and edited many more. She specializes in early literacy instruction and books for young readers, especially nonfiction.

··· About the Advisor

Dr. Shannon Cannon is a teacher educator in the School of Education at UC Davis, where she also earned her Ph.D. in Language, Literacy, and Culture. She serves on the clinical faculty, supervising pre-service teachers and teaching elementary methods courses in reading, effective teaching, and teacher action research.